To Joe and Joanne
old friends

HONG KONG POEMS

香 港 詩 歌

which will, I hope, give
you a Hong Kong you
were unable to see when
you were there.
Affectionately,
Andrew

香港詩歌
姜安道、黃國彬中英文作品選

姜安道 黃國彬 著

吳兆朋 金聖華 莫詠賢 黃國彬 譯

朗斯德爾出版社
1997

Hong Kong
Poems
in English and Chinese

by

ANDREW PARKIN
AND LAURENCE WONG

with translations by

EVANGELINE ALMBERG
SERENA JIN
MOK WING-YIN
LAURENCE WONG

RONSDALE PRESS
1997

RONSDALE PRESS
3350 West 21st Avenue
Vancouver, B.C. Canada
V6S 1G7

Set in Baskerville MT, 10pt on 13.5
Typeset by Cheersan, Vancouver, B.C.
Printing: Cheersan, Vancouver, B.C.
Cover Design: Cecilia Jang
Cover Photos: Alfred Ko
Author Photo: Alfred Ko

The publisher wishes to thank the Canada Council, the Department of Heritage and the British Columbia Cultural Services Branch for their financial assistance.

Canadian Cataloguing in Publication Data

Parkin, Andrew, 1937-
    Hong Kong poems

    Text in English and Chinese.
    ISBN 0-921870-46-9

    1. Hong Kong–Poetry. I. Wong, Laurence Kwok Pun, 1946-
II. Title.
PS8581.A7623H66   1997   C811'.54   C97-910011-9
PR9199.3.P342H69   1997

獻給加拿大和香港

TO

CANADA AND HONG KONG

目　錄

CONTENTS

序言

　　本書的詩作，曾以原文發表或廣播；譯成中英文發表或廣播的，也佔其中的大多數。我和黃國彬都寫詩，自一九九三年起，每年都參加香港中文大學逸夫書院舉辦的「吐露燈」中英詩歌朗誦晚會，也在中大婦女會為我們舉辦的詩歌朗誦會朗誦過作品。於是乃有把雙方的詩作結為一集出版的構思。經過幾個月的斟酌，一九九五年我們在加拿大領事館為加拿大研究學會朗誦詩歌時，決定把構思付諸實行。當時，我們已經看過彼此的不少作品，知道這些作品在契合之餘，又有很大的不同。此外，由於我們都是移居加拿大的人，在香港生活，在香港工作，認識後乃有他鄉遇故知之感。黃國彬在香港出生，籍貫是中國，移居加拿大後再度返港；我雖然不在香港出生，卻也是個「返港」之人，因為在六十年代，我曾在香港生活，在香港工作。

　　本書的緣起，有如上述。

　　本書作品的譯者，包括黃國彬本人，都是文學翻譯界的表表者，也是香港翻譯學會會員，中英文著作都十分豐富。

　　香港的中國文化有強烈的西方色彩，常能引發港人和居港外籍人士錯綜複雜的情懷。本書的作者和譯者，希望書中作品多少有助於中英文讀者了解這種情懷。香港的人，都像我和黃國彬那樣，經常在加拿大、中國、歐洲、東南亞之間往來。在香港，無論你住在哪裡，通常都可以看到或高或低的青山，有時候還可以看到海景。在香港，雖然鬧市和衛星城鎮密集，雖然郊野不斷受城市發展的威脅，但是未開發的郊野（其中包括位於港島和新界的野生動物保護區），目前仍佔香港總面積的百分之八十左右。由於這個緣故，本書描寫自然景色的一些作品，就不完全是作者懷念既逝之美的產物了。同時，這本選集還要告訴讀者：「你看，香港就是一首詩！不可能嗎？可能的！可別讓這個現狀改變哪。」

姜安道　於香港新界
（黃國彬譯）

10

PREFACE

The poems in this book have been published or broadcast in their original languages and most of them in translation. The idea for this pairing of poets came from the fact that Andrew Parkin and Laurence Wong participated in the bilingual annual "Tolo Lights" poetry readings held at Shaw College of the Chinese University and also gave readings as a "double act" for the Chinese University Women's Organization. Having thought about this joint publishing project for a few months, they decided to go ahead with it when they met again to give a reading for the Hong Kong Association for Canadian Studies at the Commission for Canada in 1995. By this time they had seen enough of each other's work to know that they were compatible yet very different. They also felt a friendly rapport because they are both Canadians of immigrant background, living and working in Hong Kong. Whereas Laurence Wong is a Hong Kong born Chinese "returnee", Andrew Parkin, though not born in Hong Kong, is also a "returnee", since he lived and worked in the Territory in the 1960s.

The translators, including Laurence Wong himself, are all leading literary translators and are members of the Hong Kong Translation Society. They have been published widely in the Chinese literary world as well as in English.

The team responsible for this book hopes that it will help English and Chinese readers to appreciate some of the intricacies of feeling that the Chinese but very Western culture of Hong Kong provokes in locals and expatriates. People come and go, like the poets, between Canada and China, Europe and South East Asia. Wherever one lives here there is usually a view of green hills or mountains, and sometimes the sea. Cities and the smaller towns may teem, yet there still remains about eighty percent of undeveloped countryside, including public wildlife parks in Hong Kong and the New Territories, though countryside is threatened by development on a continuing basis. Scenes of nature, then, in some of these poems aren't mere nostalgia for vanished beauty. This collection is also saying, "Look, Hong Kong is a poem! Unlikely? True! Keep it this way."

Andrew Parkin
New Territories, Hong Kong.

寄跑馬地的明信片

一個郵筒在經月的霪雨中滴著水，
並且吞下這張溫哥華明信片。
陽光下，明信片給空山添上光澤。
去了哪裡呢？油麻地的人群
和銅茶壺，以及輝煌的燈飾店。
那些燈飾店，在電車壅塞的街道兩邊羅列。
去了哪裡呢？跑馬地看賽馬的人群
和雷動崩騰向終點的獨贏馬匹。
真懷念那根晾衣竹竿，
把家中的 T 恤和裙子如飄揚的旗幟
從窄廈的窗戶晾出去。
那些大廈，我們這些孩子也嫌窄呀。
沒有盼你在這邊，只盼我在那邊。

唉，有一天，
這片零落的楓葉
會飄回跑馬地，
添上一暈香港紅。

POST CARD TO HAPPY VALLEY

A mailbox drips in the month-long rain
and swallows this Vancouver card
glossing empty mountains in the sun.
Where are the crowds of Yau Ma Tei
and brass tea urns, bright chandelier shops
lining tram-clogged streets?
Where are the Happy Valley race crowds
roaring home winners?
I miss the bamboo washing-poles
flying family tee shirts and skirts like flags
from windows in narrow tenements
cramped even to us kids.
Wish not you here, but me there.

Yes! One day this fallen maple leaf
will flutter back to Happy Valley
and turn a Hong Kong shade of red.

在啓德國際機場降落

島嶼附著海
是綠的、褐的貝殼
周邊環繞著沙
看似帽貝與藤壺
吸附著漆得光滑的、松石色的
海洋外殼。

我們一降千呎
本似蹺起的著漆外殼
實為南中國海，現又變成一匹弄皺了的絲綢
上面泛著數十艘船隻
尾部披上白色的羽毛。

我們向岩緣跌落
又及時把大陸傾斜
看到那海膽似的城市
背上的玻璃刺指著龐然紅日。

我們猝然下撲，海面漁船帆影搖動，甲板左右傾斜
輪子在焦膠噴出的煙霧裡轉動
然後在長長的有如禮堂地毯的跑道上著陸。

我漫遊於夕陽城
當空是一灣纖細的角
是月芽兒躺在太平山頂下。

商業廣告的方塊字變成霓虹蘭花
在符號星座裡的每一條街道上排列。

吹玻璃的在一條後巷的工場裡
把白熱的長管扭折，把弄着他的工藝
造成那纏在財富發電機上
一綑一綑的五彩電線。

DESCENT TO KAI TAK INTERNATIONAL AIRPORT

Islands stick to the sea
green or brown shells
sanded around the edge
limpets and barnacles it seems
sucking the smooth turquoise paint job
of the ocean's hull.

We fall hundreds of feet
and no longer upturned painted hull,
the South China Sea becomes a ruffled silk
where flocks of ships have perched
to drape their long white feathers astern.

We fall towards a rock's edge
and tip the continent aslant
finding the sea urchin city
pointing glass spines at the huge reddened sun.

We swoop above the lurching decks of shadowed junks
and then wheels spin with a puff of burnt rubber
on the long hall carpet of tarmac.

I wander the sunset city
under that thinnest horn of moon
that lies on its back below the Peak.

The characters of commerce become neon orchids
sprouting along every street in the galaxy of signs.

The glass blower twists white-hot tubes
in a back street workshop. He plies an art
of coloured coils and circuits
in the wired dynamo of wealth.

我的詩

我的詩是一道橋，沉默，寂寞，
在悠悠的歲月裏渡淳樸的族人，
幫他們涉水，登山，在黃昏和早晨
伸向曙色和炊煙中的村落。

我的詩是一口井，古老，孤獨，
世世代代在村中聽燕去燕來，
看村民在井邊浣衣洗菜，
聽跫音消失後傳來另一些腳步。

我的詩是一首歌，遙遠，持久，
藏在萬壑，藏在大海的呼吸；
當擾攘潰散，吶喊和叫囂靜止，
就裊裊揚起，像風中的海鷗。

我的詩是一顆星，夐邈，堅定，
在光年以外的廣漠抗拒酷寒。
夜深，當大氣不再遭霓虹污染，
光芒就脈脈流入仰望的眼睛。

一九七八年三月二十九日

MY POEM

My poem is a lonely, quiet bridge;
it bears through the long, long years my tribe, a simple people,
helps them cross rivers, climb hills; morning and evening
it reaches out to the village, through smoke, in the light of dawn.

My poem is an old and lonely well;
it listens down the ages to swallows as they come and go,
it watches people wash and cook nearby,
listens to footsteps as they depart, as they approach.

My poem is a song, distant, lingering,
hidden in the countless gorges, in the breathing of the sea;
when crowds disperse, cries and clamour subside,
it rises weightless, like a sea-gull in the wind.

My poem is a distant, constant star,
resisting the indifferent cold in the void beyond light years.
Deep in the night, when dark is no longer tainted by neon,
its brightness will remain in eyes that look up to the sky.

香港短歌

在山巒後面
掠過大埔的高樓
閃電晃夜空
有如白熱的龍舌
驚雷響處是中華

HONG KONG TANKA

Behind the hills
across from Taipo's towers
lightning flicks night sky
with a dragon's white-hot tongue.
Thunder rolls in from China.

中年

在河邊習泳時，
以為整條大河可以握在掌中。
到了河心，失去了方向，
才知道水闊浪寬，
湍急的暗流狡獪而陰險，
一切都不由我作主。
到了河心，我才知道，
無論怎樣掙扎，怎樣熟讀水文，
有一天，仍要觸到大漩渦的黑唇，
並且在高速的眩暈中，
沿險滑透明的峭壁
墜入寂靜的深淵。

一九九二年五月二十七日

MIDDLE AGE

When I was learning to swim near the river bank,
I thought I could hold all the river in my hands.
Only now, losing my bearings in mid-stream,
do I realize the river and its waves are broad,
that rapid undercurrents are sly and treacherous,
and that nothing is for me to decide.
Only in mid-stream do I realize
that no matter how hard I may struggle,
no matter how well-versed I may be in hydrology,
one day I will feel the lips of the huge whirlpool
and be swept at vertiginous speed
against its perilous, slippery, transparent cliff
into the abyss of silence.

27 May 1992

太空人

學童和上班的父母
丟下這潔淨的西岸郊區。
我和生活之間的聯繫——
街角的郵筒——
在我靈魂的灰色空無裡
一日復一日地滴著雨。

我剖開航空郵簡，打開
女王年輕的頭顱所枕的藍底。
藍底上，紫荊到處
在含苞待放：總督府；
九龍的鐘樓；海港——
填窄了的浴缸，上面浮動著玩具；
立法局大樓迴盪著新聲；
維多利亞港，叫陰莖般的碑石包圍；
碑石叫財富抹得油亮光鮮。

黑字舞過紙上。
我再度登上往中環的電車，
奔過畢打街奔上皇后大道中，
和你，也和你的薄扶林朋友
到法蘭西餐廳喝咖啡、吃曲奇。
此刻，古老的希爾頓酒店和咖啡室
已經坍塌——記憶被拆，成了碎磚。

ASTRONAUT

School kids and working parents
desert these tidy West Coast suburbs.
My link with life
the mailbox at the corner,
dripping with rain day after day
in my soul's grey blank.

I slit the airmail and unfold the blue
backing the Queen's young head,
bauhinia waiting there to blossom
everywhere: Government House,
Kowloon clock tower, harbour,
narrowed tub of bobbing toys,
Legco Building, echoing with new voices,
and Victoria, surrounded by penile monuments
well-oiled with wealth.

Black characters dance across the sheet
and I'm back on the tram to Central,
haring up Pedder into Queen's
for coffee and Danish at DeliFrance
with you and your friends from Pokfulam
now the old Hilton and its coffee shop
have collapsed, rubble of demolished memories.

翻到背頁，我又和你一起
在戲院里商量，想去
灣仔的霓虹燈海中逛逛。
那裡，生命把精種潑落大街小巷。

獨自在西岸的細雨中，
手中拿著一封航空郵簡，
我聽見人群疾走的喧鬧湧過。
我莊嚴地許下諾言：

把妻子和降落傘孩子空運到護照之國，
再飛回來，一個太空人：回時飛過
九龍塘愛情別墅的上空，
向啟德機場潑落。
在跑馬地再租一層樓，
可以看到賽馬的一
不管我的卡拉OK心靈
每方寸要付多少錢！

Over the page I'm with you again
in Theatre Lane planning a jaunt
to Wan Chai's neon galaxies
where life spills its seeds in alleys and streets.

Alone in soft West Coast rain
holding an airmail in my hand
I hear the roar of racing crowds.
I make my solemn vows:

fly wife and parachute kids to passport-land,
fly back, astronaut, coming in above love hotels
of Kowloon Tong for a Kai Tak splash down.
Rent a flat again in Happy Valley
with a view of the races,
whatever the cost per square inch
to my karaoke soul!

翠鳥

早春，在魚塘的上空
懸著，像一顆藍星
俯照玻璃。
把小魚祟入褐瞳，
天地眩轉間如紫電下擊。
當它掠水而去，
黑喙已叼著獵物，
朱紅的利爪收斂，
只留下一聲尖叫，
如刀劃破春曉。

一九七八年五月十五日

26

THE KINGFISHER

In early spring, hovering over
a fish pond, like a blue star
shining upon a sheet of glass,
it spellbinds a small fish
in the gaze of its brown pupils
and, dazzling the sky and earth,
strikes like purple lightning.
When it flies away, skimming the water,
the sharp vermilion claws folded,
already holding its prey in its black beak,
it leaves behind only a shrill scream
that rips open the dawn of spring.

颱風

颱風呼嘯而至
酩酊醉漢返家
敲窗捶門
渲泄漲滿的膀胱。

雲卷翻騰
閃銀帶黑
停泊處舢舨帆船躍動。

巨靈之爪撕裂
拉扯、扭曲、拔出
林木的綠髮。

肢解的竹棚
剝落如癲狂的框架
鑲嵌橙眼的路燈。

風到處拍打
它那粗糙的濕帆布
一陣玻璃利箭
乘著斜雨襲來。

心啊！你碎裂時
在一片死寂前
恰似如此。

TYPHOON

The typhoon roars in
a drunk come home
banging windows and doors
venting an enormous bladder.

Cloud coils writhe
silver and black.
At anchor sampans and junks buck.

Unseen talons rip
pull twist wrench out
the green hair of the trees.

Amputated bamboo scaffolds
peel away in a crazy lattice
frame the orange-eyed lamps.

Wind everywhere flaps
its coarse wet canvas
and a flight of glass arrows
rides the horizontal rain.

Heart, when you break
chaos will crash and crow
before the silence.

拉二胡

一個房間，
中央坐一個人，
抱一個二胡，
拉著拉著，
就拉出了高山流水。

那人坐在宇宙的中央，
繼續拉著二胡；
高山流水，
流向四方上下，
流入了過去未來。

那人不見了，
剩下二胡
在宇宙的中央
奏著高山流水。

二胡不見了，
剩下高山流水
在宇宙裡流。

一九七八年八月十八日

PLAYING THE ERHU

A room,
in the centre sits a man
holding an erhu,
drawing, drawing his bow.
He draws out tall mountains and flowing streams.

The man sits in the centre of the universe,
bowing the strings of the erhu;
tall mountains and flowing streams
flow up and down, to the four corners,
flow into the past, into the future.

The man is gone,
leaving the erhu
in the centre of the universe
to draw out tall mountains and flowing streams.

The erhu is gone,
leaving the tall mountains and flowing streams
to flow through the universe.

[Note: The erhu is a traditional Chinese two-stringed fiddle with a fixed
bow, which is intertwined with the strings.]

愛在薄暮

遠處的一層暮靄
把大埔幢幢高樓的
萊茵石燈裹起。

長長的列車軋軋
拖著載滿貨物的車廂
穿過一天將盡的時辰。

下面，村子在打呵欠；
在黑夜即將歸來之前，
昏暗的門口張開。

大海是一塊磨過的石板。
車輛沿板邊滑過，無蹤無影──
除了閃爍的眼睛。

當群犬開始狺狺不歇，吠叫到天亮，
黑暗在它的布帛裡
把象牙和尖角的所有夢幻包起。〔譯者註〕

我們雖曾見多識廣，
此刻卻孤陋寡聞，
在愛情最輕柔的觸摸中，
發現了智慧。

一九九一年六月

〔譯者註〕在西方傳說中，象牙和角是夢之所由出，兩者分
司虛幻和實際。

32

LOVE AT DUSK

A distant fog at dusk
wraps up the rhinestone lights
of Tai Po's towers.

The long trains trundle
loaded carriages
through day's last hours.

Below the village yawns;
dim doorways gape
before the prompt return of night.

The sea's a polished slate.
Along its edge the traffic slides
unseen, except for gleaming eyes.

As dogs begin to bark and bark again till light,
the darkness folds within its cloth
all dreams of ivory and horn.

We who know so little,
though once we knew so much,
discover wisdom
in love's lightest touch.

June 1991

小夜曲的聯想

一

弦聲如水；
我隨波而去，
漂過時間，
像一葉星槎，
航入了銀河。

二

夏夜的百合，
細細的，
一瓣一瓣
向我開啓，
直至玉蕊。

一九七三年五月七日

FREE ASSOCIATIONS ON A SERENADE

I

The strings sound like water.
I drift with the ripples
beyond time
like the celestial boat
sailing into the Silver River.

II

Tenderly,
petal upon petal,
a lily opens to me
on a summer night,
until its jade pistil is revealed.

[Note: In Chinese mythology the celestial boat is a raft that sails
between the stars, while the Silver River is the Milky Way.]

在下臨吐露港的山上

火車嚓啦啦地相逢，經過，
遠遠地，靠著下面的海岸
相逢，經過。
在這樣濕潤的下午，
海是一塊拉開的灰布。

我繼續上攀，越過
露出地面的巖層。
巖層巍巍，高出
那獲得許可的未來。
獲得許可的未來
由計劃者，以及由選舉
或委任產生的議員，
以及律師，以及整群的建築師、
工程師、工程估計員、會計師批准。
我已經聽到卡嗒砰磅
由更多的建設工程響起—
其實是破壞過去的地方感。

這段短暫的時間賣掉了，
賣掉了再賣，一如土地—
我們僅有的地球。

在這壁陡峭的巖石上，
儘管他日帶來震蕩，
大自然還在咧嘴而笑。
因為，穿過歲月和天氣，
一絲羞赧的綠意纏著裂縫，
搖著纖小的喇叭瓣—
堂堂皇皇的深紅。

突然，我煞有介事。
我雖然凡軀無寄，須臾間
卻有賓至如歸之感。

ON A MOUNTAIN ABOVE TOLO HARBOUR

Chuntering trains meet and pass
meet and pass far down by the shore:
in this moist afternoon
the sea's a stretched grey cloth.

I climb further up beyond a rocky outcrop
high above the permitted future
approved by planners, legislators,
elected or not, and the lawyers
and the whole pack of architects,
engineers, quantity surveyors, accountants,
and I can hear already the clatter and thump
of yet more construction
really the destruction of a previous sense of place.

And this brief time is sold,
sold over and over again
like the land, our only earth.

On sheer rock, nature grins
despite the shock time future brings,
for through time and weather
a shy green wisp clings in a cleft
and waves minuscule trumpet petals
of deep red heraldry.

Suddenly there's a sense of occasion.
For a few seconds, human and rootless,
I feel welcome.

雨夜狂想

簷前的雨水在滴,
滴到所有的人都入睡,
滴到一切聲音結束,
把一天的星光滴熄。
那時,宇宙就會像個空靈的貝殼,
只有黑簷下的淅瀝在裡面迴盪。

RHAPSODY ON A RAINY NIGHT

Rain drips from the eaves,
drips, till the world sleeps,
drips, till all sound dies,
quenching every star in the sky.
Now the universe is a shell,
ethereal chamber wherein echo only
water beads dripping from the dark eaves.

在中文大學

在陡峭得出奇的斜坡上，
因蟬聲而刺耳的葉叢
隱藏著神鳥。
神鳥的龍翼化爲蕨叢，
矛刃似的銳爪化爲細枝。

鷹喙鷹舌的鳳鳥哇，
在年老和年輕的心中
築起火焰之巢吧——
那吐露港上的燈塔——
並成爲九位智慧天使的標誌。

一九九一年春

AT CHINESE UNIVERSITY

On curiously abrupt slopes
foliage sharp with cicadas
hides the famous bird,
its dragon wings become ferns,
pike blade claws twigs.

Feng, with eagle beak and tongue,
build the nest of flames
in minds old and young,
beacon above the sea at To Lo,
and signal nine angels of wisdom.

Spring 1991.

永樂大鐘 並序

　　永樂大鐘，素有鐘王之稱，爲世界上數一數二的大鐘。明永樂年間鑄造，高六‧七五米，底口外徑三‧三米，重四萬六千六百餘斤，鐘面刻有楷書經文二十二萬七千多字，聲音可傳至四十五公里外，目前仍烏亮如新。現存於北京大鐘寺。

當小鑼和小鈸爭鳴，
你是靜止的天河，
沉默於時間的夜空。
你像唐古拉山脈，
把瞿塘峽的咆哮
收入各拉丹多的冰川。
像一條大江，澎湃奔湧間凝結，
波聲驟停如出擊的騎兵
六百年前突然勒馬。
又如珊瑚紅的貝殼，星光下
收起沙灘的軟浪和細漪。
六百年來，你的聲音
是蟄伏在萬尋之下的黑濤，
比海藻間的暖流還要寂靜。
到小鑼和小鈸一一力竭，
所有的耳朵厭倦了噪音，
你才像個巨人醒轉，
拂去虬髯上的青苔，
伸腰，仰首，一吐一納間，
所有的耳朵聽見了天河下瀉，
聽見黑雷在萬壑竄逐奔騰。
在一萬尺的高空，
冷杉濤回應著月夜的潮湧。

THE GREAT BELL OF YONGLE

Small gongs and cymbals may vie with each other,
but you are the River of Heaven, a stilled flow,
quiet in time's night sky.
Like the Tanggula Mountains,
you gather the roar of Qutang Gorge
into the glaciers of Geladandong;
like a mighty river, frozen in thundering surge,
billows abruptly checked; like a cavalry charge
from six hundred years ago suddenly reined to a halt;
like a coral-pink shell in starlight,
drawing in soft waves and ripples that lap upon sand.
For six hundred years, your voice
has been a dark wave
a thousand fathoms deep,
quieter than the warm current that slips between seaweed.
When small gongs and cymbals have worn themselves out
and every ear is weary of noise,
then you will awaken, a gaint,
wiping moss from your curling whiskers,
stretching yourself, lifting your head.
At each breath
every ear will hear a cataract from the River of Heaven,
dark thunderbolts stampeding in a myraid valleys.
In the highest firmament
the billowing firs will roar, echoing the surging tide of the
          moonlit night.

沱沱河直撲瞿塘的大水
回應著大平原疾馳的鐵騎。
然後，雷聲漸去
漸遠；波聲和蹄聲消失；
冷杉濤隨北風逝入燕山；
海潮緩緩，緩緩地退減；
星光下，一枚珊瑚紅的貝殼，
在發光的沙灘
細細斟出夏夜的暖漪。

一九八二年一月二十日

Hurtling headlong into the Qutang Gorge, the Tuotuo River
will echo the cavalry charging across the vast plain.
Thunder will gradually fade and die.
Waves and rumbling of hoofs will fade away.
The fir-billowing north wind
will vanish into the Yan Mountains.
Slowly, slowly the tide will ebb.
And in the starlight, a coral-pink shell on a gleaming strand
will gently pour out warm ripples of a summer night.

20 January 1982

[Note: This bell, called the King of Bells, cast in the Yongle period of the Ming Dynasty, stands 6.75 metres high and weighs over 23,300 kilograms. It is housed in the Temple of the Great Bell in Beijing. Scriptures of over 227,000 characters in regular script are engraved on its surface. The bell can be heard at distances of more than 45 kilometres.]

拼圖
（獻給梁秉中教授）

關節錯綜的謎
經年累月演變爲
痛苦的拼圖

外科大夫在肌膚上的紫圖
以小點及大弧
在膝蓋上開路

靈巧的指，穩定的手
藏於手套內層
面罩上雙目凝神

專注的笑容
當他重新安排膝蓋的拼圖
手術室中人人注目

剪去的紅、白軟骨
刷掉的堊狀碎片
變成病人殘遺之物

骨頭修剪鑽孔
皮膚重連痊癒
精緻的切口縫合如淺淺的笑容。

JIGSAW
(for Professor P.C. Leung)

A joint's involved puzzle
over the years becomes
a jigsaw of pain

a surgeon's purple sketch on skin
with a dot and bold curve
marks the way into the knee

adroit fingers, steady hands
inside gloves' other skin
vigilant eyes above the mask

a smile of concentration
and the theatre team all focus
as he realigns the puzzle pieces of a knee

snipped cartilage pink and white
scoured chalky fragments
become the patient's relics

bones pruned and drilled
skin resewn to recover
and that elegant cut stitched like a thin smile.

僵硬的膝蓋傷口作痛。
她在椅間跛行
於桌上展開拼圖
當關節癒合肌肉復原時
把這另一幅圖畫拼合，
病後護理的小心鍛煉。

他操剪拉出
一條打圈的長線
扭曲而出似最後的問號

而我們對此回春妙術報以一笑
他以一己的生命賦予眾生
另一個機會踏足曲折的道路。

一九九四年十月

48

The wound aches in the patient's stiffened knee.
She limps from chair to chair
spreads a jigsaw on a table

putting this other picture back together
as joints mend muscles gather strength,
careful exercise of after-care.

He snips and pulls
one long looped stitch
twitched out like a last coiled question

and we smile at this gift of healing:
his life affords so many different lives
another chance to walk their spiral paths.

October 1994.

秋懷

這時候，吐露港又是
水痕靜摺，老鷹高飛了。
潔白的浪花，悠閒地
為港中的眾嶼鑲邊。
秋風沾著陽光的琥珀
從草山那邊吹來，
輕搖著樟樹灘的蘆葦；
在海港最藍處
飄起幾隻白鷗；
把馬鞍山和烏溪沙的輕霧
吹出赤門海峽之外；
把更遠的海、更遠的山
吹入老鷹的視程。
這時候，船灣淡水湖
浸著八仙嶺的倒影，
會藍得更深、更涼。
在明山、靜海、和高天中，
宇宙也更廣更靜了；
白露過後，一直隨雁聲擴闊。
這時候，該躺在舢舨上讓吐露港輕搖；
或在船灣堤上聽寂靜的秋聲；
在大學站懶洋洋地靠著長椅，
不管柴油火車是否會準時到達；
或在中大之巔的新亞，
挨著水塔遠望大埔的漁村；
然後閉目、仰首向著暖陽……

睜眼，見電車外
滿街凋傷的紅葉
已開始轉黃，
我才瞿然驚覺，
此身是真的
離開吐露港了。

一九八六年十月十一日

50

AUTUMN THOUGHTS

Now Tolo Harbour spreads
its gentle ripples while the eagles fly on high.
Languid white foam
fringes the haven's scatter of islets.
Autumn winds, tinted with amber sunlight,
blow from grassy hills across the bay
and gently shake the reeds by Camphor Beach.
From the bluest part of the harbour
a few white gulls take off.
The soft mists in Ma On Shan and Wu Kai Sha
are blown beyond Chik Mun Channel.
Now eagles can survey
the further seas, more distant hills.
The freshwater lake of Plover Cove
reflecting the Eight Fairies Hills
will be turning an even deeper and a cooler blue.
Amid fair hills, calm seas, and high heavens,
the universe will grow vaster, quieter,
expanding with the wild goose's plangent cry
                          when White Dew has gone by.
I want to lie on a sampan, letting Tolo waters gently swell,
or listen on the dam of Plover Cove to Autumn's solitary sounds,
or sit and lean languidly on a bench at University station,
not caring if the diesel train arrives on time,
or lean againts New Asia College water tower
on the hilltop of the Chinese U.,
gazing at Taipo's distant fishing villages,
and then, eyes closed, turn my head towards the warming sun...

Opening my eyes, I see desolate red leaves
already turning yellow outside my streetcar.
Suddenly I'm aware
I've forever lost the harbour at Tolo.

Toronto, Autumn 1986.

閃電拆開黑穹的針腳

閃電拆開黑穹的針腳：
破爛的廣宇
靠一條簡短的光線懸垂著。

沒有風。看不見的精靈叫你屏息，
到低沉的鼓聲隆隆不絕從北方滾來，
迴盪於黑夜空洞的耳朵才罷休。

像個聽故事的小孩，我聚精會神地
聽雨點最初的幾粒肥碩種子
播落窗戶的玻璃。

一本書，看了一半，朦朧的書頁
在等待下一灘白光潑落──陳腐的引文，
字體由暴風雨照亮，載於更龐大的卷帙。

巨大的字體橫越變化不斷的天空──
一份份寫了又抹、抹了又寫的文稿，
記錄著一次又一次的失敗談判。

巨大的字體草擬著虛榮的獨白，
拆開王朝一個個的衛士，
敘述著政權的氣焰。

雙軌在鋼質的微笑中
轉彎。前進時，電氣化火車
在上面來回穿過黑夜

穿過國土的大騷動，
前進時織拆着
卑微乘客的無聲期盼。

電閃把它的字體
粗縫過中國上空的黑布。

LIGHTNING UNSTITCHES THE DARK SKY

Lightning unstitches the dark sky;
great tattered heavens hang
by one brief thread of light.

No wind. Unseen presence hold your breath
until the muffled drumroll from the north
resounds in the cavernous ears of night.

Attentive as a child at story time
I hear the rain's first fat seeds
broadcast on the window-panes.

The dim page of a half-read book
awaits the next white splash of light,
its storm-lit print a banal quotation in a greater text.

Huge characters across the sky
of endless change, successive palimpsests
of failed negotiations,

sketch monologues of vanity,
unseam dynastic champions,
narrate the arrogance of power.

On twin tracks curved
in a steely smile
electric trains shuttle through the night

thread through the country's great to-do
stitching and unstitching as they go
the silent yearnings of their lowly passengers.

Lightning bastes its characters
across the charcoal cloth of China's sky.

只要你站得久

只要你站得久，
像一株清癯的竹；
看似經不起風雨，
人人回家，或者去趁熱鬧，
或者怕黑，畏冷，
你仍然一個人靜立著，
默看一山的楓樹隨風變紅，
風，是不會吹得太久的。

只要你站得久，
風會停，黲黷會消散，
剩下晴地朗天
把你包容；
看你留著昔日的面貌，
不懼，不憂，也不喜；
只有冬去春來時輕微的哀傷。

只要你站得久，
雲會散，眾星會濾出清光，
滴落你的銀髮，
滴落你輕微的哀傷。
而那時是冬去春來，
眾樹都離開了你，
不知所終了。

一九八七年一月十日

JUST STAND THERE LONG ENOUGH

Just stand there long enough –
one slender bamboo spray
too frail for wind, for rain –
and, when everyone's joined the crowd for fun
or gone home dreading the dark or cold,
you stay, standing alone, quietly
watching maples along the hills turn red with the wind.
Winds – they never blow too long.

Just stand there long enough,
and wind will fall, all haze vanish,
leaving but earth's beauty and clear sky
as your setting:
to see you, your face as it was before,
showing no fear, no grief, no joy
but a hint of sadness that spring is at hand, winter in retreat.

Just stand there long enough,
and clouds dissolve, while clear light, filtered through stars,
drips on your silver threads,
drips on your tinge of sadness.
By then, winter will have gone and spring arrived.
You're left alone, all trees gone
and no one knows where.

10 January 1987

另一·伊甸

我倆另一伊甸是座茅舍，
瀕臨大海，潮汐不息。

妳的頭髮是芬芳的庭園。
妳的聲音是空中的仙樂。
妳的雙眸澄碧
漾溢著自知與歡欣。
妳的微笑是晴空
乍現的光華。
妳的胴體是銷魂之鄉，
叫我欲離不能。

我倆另一伊甸是座茅舍，
瀕臨大海，潮汐不息。

ANOTHER EDEN

Our other Eden is a cottage,
the sea close by, eternally restless.

Your hair is a fragrant garden.
Your voice is music in the air.
Your eyes are a green shade
of self-knowledge and laughter.
Your smile is a sudden radiance
of fine weather.
Your body is an enchanted landscape
where I must live.

Our other Eden is a cottage,
the sea close by, eternally restless.

熱帶魚

園裡的天鵝絨翻唇蘭
如奶白的玉杯泛著嫩紅，
蕊內的香氣如醇酒在黑暗中滿溢。
星光下，我潛游於夏夜的海洋，
酡然撥開烏亮而柔滑的軟浪和細漪，
循熟悉的方向前進，讓無聲的暖流
漂過我的前額，最後發現兩枚仙貝，
靜藏在暖流深處，精巧玲瓏，
等一尾多情的熱帶魚游過來輕吻。

TROPICAL FISH

Velvet-leaved hetaeria in the garden:
creamy jade cup with curled lips,
suffused with delicate pink,
fragrance of its flower-heart brims like a vintage in the dark.
In the starlight, I dive beneath the summer night sea,
and, flushed with drink, brush aside the soft waves
                              and fine ripples
which shine, black and sleek.
Forward along a familiar route, the warm currents
wash silently past my brow, until at last I find two celestial shells,
exquisite, ingeniously wrought,
lying hidden, mute in the depths of warm currents,
waiting for a passionate tropical fish to glide forward
                              and gently offer kisses.

睡海

今夜，叵測的海
是一條黑龍，
與風暴鬥得筋疲力盡。

海裡，
躺著自我遭受船難後的珍寶，
靜如有毒的海藻。

陸地上，忙碌的顧客
始終喧鬧無厭。
他們蜂擁而去，消耗縮減的空氣。

破爛的天空
則炫耀荒蕪的寶石，
把它們當作星星。

一九九一年六月

SLEEPING SEA

Tonight the faithless sea
is a dark dragon
exhausted by storms.

Under the sea
lie treasures of the shipwrecked self,
quiet as toxic weeds.

On earth, the busy shoppers
always hungry and loud
swarm to consume the dwindled air.

And the tattered sky
shows off its barren gems
as if they were stars.

June 1991.

拍照

你站在樹下拍照，
樹的後面是一幢建築物，
建築物後面是一座大山，
大山之後是茫茫的大海，
大海之後是變幻的白雲，
白雲之後，是漠漠的天空；
天空之外的背景，
任攝影機的焦點怎樣推移
也尋找不到；
直至你離去，
老樹枯萎，
山海白雲全部消失，
如一襲破衣裳
漠漠的天空脫落，
最後的背景
才向無人窺視的鏡頭
裸露。

一九七六年八月三十日

62

TAKING A PICTURE

You stand under a tree, posing for a picture.
Behind the tree is a building,
behind the building is a huge mountain,
behind the mountain is the wide, wide sea,
and then white clouds, always changing,
and then the vast empty sky.
The background beyond the sky –
let the focus shift as it may –
is not to be reached
till you leave:
the tree withers,
mountain and sea and white clouds vanish,
like tattered clothes
the vast empty sky peels off,
and the ultimate background
before the lens, in the absence of the peeping eye,
bares itself.

30 August 1976

四寶

起初他們把我的筆拿走：
我就用頭髮書寫。

他們把我的紙也偷去了：
我就寫在牆上。

他們終於充公了墨和硯：
我唯有用碎骨寫血書代箋。

FOUR TREASURES

First they took my brush:
I wrote with my own hair.

They stole my paper:
I wrote on walls.

They confiscated ink and stone:
I wrote in blood with a bit of bone.

[Note: The traditional writing implements (brush, ink, stone, paper) were sometimes called the scholar's "four treasures". The fifth was a sword.]

望江南

這一年的秋天，劫灰飛盡，
我們回去時，菊花開得特別燦爛。
在久違的山齋外擺一張小桌：
你端出熱茶和新烹的蟹，
我拿出一個紋月白釉瓶
（秦火後變得更晶瑩更光潔），
為你，也為我倒一碗香醇的白酒
（這時刻，微酡該在你兩頰泛起了，
如紅霞在林外的白雪上棲遲）。

青瓷碗裡，酒聲凝寂如天池：
一聲鶴唳劃入高空：
啊，在劫灰飛盡之後
我和你，終於回到了江南，
怡然傾聽寒泉在遠山下瀉。

一九八八年十月十五日

66

GAZING SOUTH

This autumn after the calamity all the dust was blown away.
When we came back, the chrysanthemums
                        opened in greater splendour.
Outside the long-missed mountain studio we set a little table.
You brought hot tea and freshly cooked crabs
while I took a bottle, with moon pattern and white glaze
(that had turned all the brighter, clearer, for the Qin fire)
and poured out bowls of fragrant, mellow wine.
(Then your cheeks flushed with a faint glow from the drink,
the red hue of evening clouds that rest high
                        on white snows beyond the woods.)

Like Lake Tianchi, the wine in the blue-glazed bowl
                        is silent and still.
A crane's cry soars sharply into the sky.
Oh, now that the dust has blown away,
you and I, at long last, have returned to the south
and, content, can just detect
the distant roar of that cold spring
                        rushing down the mountainside.

15 October 1988

[Note: For Chinese poets, gazing south suggests gazing across from the north bank of the Yangtze River to the Southern Region in China.]

給一名巴黎女子的情書

我聽見群犬狺狺吠出妳的名字
在山谷另一邊的村落。
當鳥兒鳴唱
它唱出妳的名字。

昨日我看見一隻白鷺
駐足凝神冥想
於海傍淺灘中。

如妳一般神態雍容。

妳是這可愛的鳥兒
自柔波升起
飛越域外的叢林。

妳不曾對我承諾什麼
也從不想要求我
諾言輕許或謊話連篇。

妳對我指出
金輝穹蒼上的眾天使
而白鳥啊！

我將它們
偕同妳自身的美
擁入心坎深處。

LOVE LETTER TO A WOMAN IN PARIS

I hear the dogs bark your name
in the village across the valley.
When a bird sings
it sings your name.

Yesterday I saw a white egret
standing in the shallows of the sea
lost in contemplation.

Like you it makes a gift of elegance.

You are the lonely bird
rising from gentle waves
and flying through foreign woods.

You have promised me nothing
and never thought to demand of me
vain promises or lies.

You have shown me the angels
traced on the gold of the sky,
and white bird

I have taken them
with your own beauty
into the deepest glades of myself.

但妳永不會囚拘籠中。
妳會否在某一天破曉時分
乘那淺灰的浪濤歸來？

我會穿越四大洲
將妳遍尋
在最料想不到時發現妳

在河之畔
在稍離人群處
愛都中的白鷺。

You will never live in a cage.
Will you come back one dawn
in the grey wash of the waves?

I will search for you
across four continents
find you when least expected

on the edge of the river
a little away from the crowds,
white egret in the city of love.

春

你的眼睛，在冷夜醒來，
柔柔開啓，眼波泛向天邊。
迷濛惺忪中，子規在啼。
到眸光澄明，一隻白鷺
就從你的長睫，翩翩
飛入眸心的瀲灩。

SPRING

You woke on a cold night,
your eyes opening tenderly,
sending ripples towards the brink of heaven.
Half-awake: cuckoo song.
When the light in your eyes cleared, a stork
from your long lashes fluttered
into the heart of your pupils, brim-full.

晨光熹微時

破曉前晨光熹微時
在夜遊者尋歡作樂
喧騰返家後的沉靜中
在鳥兒出沒草地前的寥寂時刻

我打開夢境長廊
盡頭的門戶
把那夢長留身後
並調整雙目以注視那矇矓的彎弧

彎弧上妳臀部的曲線
降至腰際
再上升開展至背部
終止於我輕吻其上的幽黑肩頭。

我閉上雙目暫擁在
溫柔的恬靜中
正想遁入夢鄉
但妳卻轉身相向而我

給妳纖長的手臂摟住
正如生命中良機再逢。

一九九三年八月

IN THE LESSER DARK

In the lesser dark of the hour before dawn
in the silence after late revellers
have come noisily home
in the still hour before birds stalk the lawn

I open the doors at the end
of the long corridor of dream
that I leave forever behind
and adjust my eyes to the dim bend

where the curve of your hip
falls to your waist
and rises broadening the back
to a dark shoulder I brush with my lip.

My eyes close and I'm held
in a moment of tender calm
ready to slip away into sleep
but you turn and I'm held

by your long, slender arm,
another chance at life.

August 1993

當我的夢如無際的疆土展開

夜裡，當我的夢如無際的疆土展開，
　我只希望它有一條長長的岸線
和一個發光的沙灘在月下任暖浪輕拍，
　上面的紫貝只讓一隻纖手去挑撿。

那時，你就會航入我的海域，
　把小船靜泊灣中。赤足涉水，
在月色之下不再矜持，不再趑趄，
　讓秀美的足踝踐落我夢土的邊陲。

一九八三年三月三十一日

WHEN MY DREAM SPREADS
LIKE SOME BOUNDLESS LAND

At night,
when my dream spreads like some boundless land,
I wish for a long coastline of gleaming sand
gently washed by warm waves in the moonlight
and strewn with lilac shells, picked by one delicate hand.

And then you sail into my domain,
quietly moor your boat in a cove,
wade barefoot through the water.
Under the moon, you abandon hesitancy and restraint.
Your slender ankles shine and
                    footprints mark my dreamland's border.

31 March 1983

山巒和海港（一）

我在陽台上眺望
山巒和海港—
一切詩的父母

細滑如絲淡灰的薄霧
籠罩著無言的樹木，
拖著鬼氣沉沉的旗幟橫掃火山崗。

沿岸迢迢的長路上空
藍煙慢慢地
從花園火堆間升起

橙紅的起重機
伸著機器模型似的長嘴
指向海的上空

在喧嚷的海灣邊，火車咔嗒咔嗒響
繞過附近村落
村落裡有孩童在嬉戲

這首詩卻在腦海裡浮現
在建築地盤的塵埃中
從鎖骨上的汗珠蒸餾而成

MOUNTAIN AND HARBOUR I

On the balcony I watch
mountain and harbour,
parents of all poetry.

That grey silk mist
veils mute trees,
draws ghostly flags across volcanic hills.

High above the coast's long road
smoke climbs blue
from garden fires.

The orange crane
angles a meccano beak
above the sea.

Trains clatter by the cluttered bay
and curve beside the village
where the children play.

But the poem grows in the mind's
envisaging, in dusty building sites,
distilled from sweatbead skin on collar-bones,

它的節奏是手操鑿岩機的嘎啦格格
和苦力的回音
是打入基柱的重擊砰砰

它的韻律卻跳躍自
小販們叫賣的公式
或源自小孩的口齒

它的滋味是
竹棚工人用力甩動台架時
汗流浹背的鹽

它有魚乾的氣味，它的基調
是酒吧女郎在霓虹燈下
通宵達旦的妖冶衣裳

its rhythms are rattling jack hammers
and echoing coolies,
thud of the driven piles

its rhyming leaps
from hawkers' shouted formulae
or springs from children's lips

its taste is the salt
of sweat on the backs of bamboo scaffoldmen
as they lash the cage

its smell is dried fish, its mood
the tarty clothes of bar girls
sleepless amid night's neon signs.

山巒和海港（二）

「山巒和海港對我之容忍，」
有如親生父母，智者說道：
世上每一首詩都由他們孕育。」

「多少詩不都在這兒
在這山和海之間
這小巷錯綜、商店林立的地方成長？

這些詩的卵子產於灣仔的
舊鼠窩還是旺角的街市？
在深水埗的群鬼間

還是九龍塘的陰暗消沉的別墅？
這些詩的音調可洋溢於快活谷？
每個意象可都彼此包孕？

把你的秘密
你從經濟公屋和圍牆村屋
贏取到的秘密傳給我吧。」

「沒有秘密，」
智者笑道：
「一切都已說出，都已唱誦。」

「然而……」

MOUNTAIN AND HARBOUR II

"Mountain and harbour endure me
as my true parents," says the sage,
"and they conceive every poem in the world."

"How many poems grow here
between mountain and harbour
in the litter of alleys and shops?

Are they spawned in the old rat runs
of Wanchai or the markets of Mongkok,
among the ghosts in Shamshuipo,

in shadowy langour of villas in Kowloon Tong?
Is their tone alive in Happy Valley?
Is each image carved curling within another?

Tell me your secrets,
won from tenements
and the tiled village houses with their walls."

"There are no secrets,"
smiles the sage.
"All has been said and sung."

"And yet . . . "

寂寞

寂寞是禪房闃然，
黃昏時雨水在簷前淅瀝。

寂寞是深秋中沙灘的腳印，
只有風聲、潮聲飄過。

寂寞是無人的渡口，
斜照落在木橋上的贈詞。

寂寞是你，秋風中，
在漸涼的陽光下看顫楊翻閃。

SOLITUDE

Solitude is a room in a Buddhist monastery,
quiet at dusk, with rain dripping from the eaves.

Solitude is footprints on a beach in the depth of Autumn,
with only the sound of wind and drifting tide.

Solitude is a deserted ferry crossing,
where the setting sun shines upon parting words
                              on a wooden bridge.

Solitude is you, standing in the Autumn wind,
Looking at an aspen that quivers and glimmers
                              in the cooling sun.

港畔（一）

她們的嗓子，名不經傳的女人，
沙啞地，在船上、在田野間、
在花園裡和工地上發聲。

聲音來自村屋的內院，
來自擠塞的斗室，
來自搖動的舢板，

以求遺產傳之後世，
好讓巾幗兒女吐氣揚眉。

HARBOURSIDE I

Voices of unwritten women,
hoarse from boats and fields
gardens and building sites,

speak from the inner courts
of village houses or cramped spaces,
speak in the rocking sampans,

seeking a heritage to hand on,
letting girl children thrive.

港畔（二）

逝者的幽靈、喪家的悲傷
悼念往黃金西岸一去不返的親人
他們群集於曾幾何時的上環街市
在已匿跡的貨倉裡、埋在新街道下的舊碼頭上
響往於油漬斑斑的浪濤的拍岸聲
在帶鹽的海風裡靜坐
這是看不出的鬼域，新客不會留神。

有人記得當年的俄國船載著契可夫——
一位想目睹一切的大夫，
他想見到進步、貿易、
博物館和新道路
以及通往山頂的軌道。

這個奇蹟，由遠別了整齊的郊區的英人
與逃離了劫後祖國的漢人所創，
在短短數代間建設了新的事物。
身在奇蹟裡，有人想起征服者，
想起旭日的火焰，
想起被毆打群逐的囚俘
或被狂傲者摧殘的女性，
又想起因吐痰而給撩上手銬還遭鞭策的鬚眉。

鬼魂群集在記憶網中顛簸擺動
一次復一次被網拖走
又再拋回浪濤中，投進垂死的海——
此時此地駕馭漁船的活人的海。

HARBOURSIDE II

The souls of the Hong Kong dead, of sad families
of the lost who left for the golden west,
they throng in once-upon-a-time Western Market
in vanished godowns, on old quays buried by new streets
and yearn still for the slap of oily waves
and sit calmly here in salt sea air
of haunts unseen, unheeded by the new.

Some remember the Russian ship carrying Chekhov,
a doctor wanting to see it all,
the progress, the trade,
the museum and new roads,
a railway up to the peak.

In the miracle worked by English far from tidy suburbs
and by Chinese fleeing chaos, repeated rape of the motherland,
to build something new in so few generations,
some remember the conquerors,
fires from a rising sun,
and the herding of beaten prisoners
or the arrogant taking of women to be used
and the goading of men chained through the hands for spitting.

Ghosts throng and thrash in the nets of memory
trawled again and again.
Ghosts are thrown back into the waves of the dying sea
of the living who ride the machine of the here and now.

發跡致富的人大興土木築起樓房，
有花園和月門
那兒會有鬼魂趁烏雲蔽星之際起舞
在雲層裡會有鬼魂走在船夫拋上岸的繩纜

（儘管帝國末日的諧劇上演，
權力交替貪婪無厭：
自以為是的暴發戶，沾沾自喜、
來自少年世界的洋人又奈何？）。

同時，這城市、海港和島嶼
在這燦爛的思潮競逐裡閃光。

Those who grow rich will build houses
with gardens and moon gates
where ghosts will dance when the stars hide behind clouds
where ghosts will walk on a line a ferryman throws ashore

(despite the farce of empire's end
the greed-filled transition of power
the smug new-rich and self-satisfied foreigners
from an adolescent world)

while city and harbour and islands
gleam in the bright tide-race of thought.

大寒

在血管裡，破冰船
陷入了絕境，
大雪後的天空冷藍欲裂，
陽光向大地狠擲著削膚的冷刃，
擊落眼鏡框和車窗的冷金屬時
我聽見冰窟的金鋼鑽切著金鋼鑽。
在風刀雪劍下向地平竄逃，
要撲入大化的洪爐，
跳入紅光閃閃的鋼水裡沐浴，
卻被風刀追到絕域，面如死灰時
墜入一百萬年前熄滅的餘燼。
天空坼裂了，在等待一萬座火山
以熔巖捲起一場海嘯，
等洶洶的熱浪暖潮
沖走冥王星外的黑冷，
卻只聽到所有的星系
在冥王星外凍裂，
最後剩下天狼的青鋒，
把宇宙如一幅黑帛切斷。

GREAT COLD

Inside my blood vessels an ice-breaker
faces an impasse.
After heavy snow, the sky's cold and blue as if ready for blasting.
And the sun is wielding cold flaying-knives against the earth.
When the sun's blades hit the cold metal
of spectacles or car windows,
I hear diamond cutting diamond in the cold's great abyss.
Dodging wind-knives and snow-swords, I make for the horizon
to leap into a bowl of molten steel flashing red –
but caught up and trapped by blades of wind, I look ashen grey
then fall into the ashes of a fire that died a million years ago.
The sky is ripped apart, waiting for ten thousand volcanoes
to retch up a tidal wave of molten lava
so that surging heat waves and warm tides
can wash away the cold dark beyond Pluto –
instead I hear all the galaxies
freeze and crack,
leaving at last only the green blade of Sirius
to cut the universe in two like a length of black silk.

四季卷軸
　——致劉國松

四季的卷軸展開
感情的地形圖
和從天而降的白色細縷——
自宇宙穹頂飄落的雪花。
在已經發芽的
枯樹堆中，
你聽得到眾鳥的喉嚨
發出無聲的鳴叫。
而這時候，春天像個小孩，
到處蹦跳嬉耍，
在夏天把彩色絲巾
鋪過陡峭的斜坡前，
測試世界。
不過，我已經是秋天，
隨時可以讓畫家的筆
塗抹成熟的歲月，
並且收割豐盛的年華。
而這時候，一把把
懸垂於冬穹的白縷
會從高處下拋，成爲港灣。
港灣內，世界會再度定幀。

一九九一年三月

94

THE FOUR SEASONS HANDSCROLL
(for Liu Kuo-sung)

the scroll of seasons unfurls
a relief map of the feelings
and fall of sky in tiny white curls
flakes from the universal roof
and in the ruins of trees
already in bud
you can hear silent calls
from the throats of birds
as Spring romps everywhere
like a child
testing the world
before Summer spreads its shawl
of coloured silk across abrupt slopes
but I am Autumn
ready for the artist's brush
to spread the ripened days
and harvest a rich life
when the world freeze-frames again
in a haven of handfuls hurled
of white curls hung in a Winter sky

March 1991

[Note: Liu Kuo-sung (born 1932) is one of the best known Hong
Kong painters, now retired and living in Taiwan. An idea of the
range of his Chinese modernity may be gained from *The
Restrospective of 60-year-old Liu Kuo-sung* (Taichung: Taiwan Mu-
seum of Art, 1992).]

狂吟

讓蘆葦諂媚任性的風吧；
我是山脈，
劃出風的道路。

讓海藻奉承善變的潮汐吧；
我是月亮，
支配潮汐的漲退。

讓磁石服從嚴峻的南北吧；
我是大地，
因我才有方向。

一九七六年十二月二十八日

RAVING SONG

Let reeds pander to the wayward wind.
I am the mountain range
that determines the course of the wind.

Let seaweed flatter the inconstant tide.
I am the moon
that controls the water's ebb and flow.

Let magnets swing and bow to unbending North and South.
I am the great earth:
only I have directions.

28 December 1976

非法移民之歌

我要離開了，離開這地方！
我要離開了，掌握像樣點的生活！
我要擺脫這些宣傳勞什子。
這些勞什子真叫精神蒙羞淪喪。

希望和信仰已經來日無多，
我得逃離銅鑼和跑錶，
躲避只懷一胎的新娘！
我要給蛇頭付錢，好摸黑去香港過活。

到了香港，我會住在目眩的高處，
或在某一多塵的樓梯下打瞌睡，
或在荒村的巷子裡徘徊，
或在建築工地幹活，住在裡面的小屋。

箭豬城裡，憑混凝土脊骨的承載，
我會攀爬一個個竹棚。
到了新年，我會登山
找一個活像你的女孩！

在陰暗處，我縫補我的襯衫，
為針插之城乾杯。
我會遇見一個滿身芳香的摩登女郎。
他有錢而漂亮，個性生來浪漫。

SONG OF AN ILLEGAL IMMIGRANT

I'll hit the road and quit this place!
I'll hit the road and grab a better life!
I'll skip the propaganda sores
that bring the spirit to disgrace.

I'll shun the stopwatch and the gong
as time runs out on hope and faith
and dodge the one-child-bearing brides!
I'll pay a snakehead for the night trip to Hong Kong.

And there I'll live at a dizzy height
or under some dusty staircase doze
or prowl abandoned village streets
or work from a shed on a building site.

I'll scale the scaffolds of bamboo
on a concrete spine in a porcupine town
and at New Year I'll climb the hills
to search for a girl that's just like you!

And under the shade I'll mend my shirt
and drink a toast to the pin cushion town.
I'll meet a sweet-smelling modern girl
who's pretty and rich and born to flirt.

即使在日漸縮小的郊野，
她穿上綠色的運動衣仍不減苗條；
他的運動鞋呀，比農村
新娘的任何嫁妝都要貴些。

陽光轉暗時我會在城中的街上溜躂。
我會把長長的香煙叼在齒間啜吸。
我頸上會掛著純金的項鏈；
項鏈上，有她心形的玉墜懸掛。

我會把手提電話用得嫻熟。
我會帶一疊大牛，卻沒有身分證。
我們的孩子會到外國唸書。
可是，我們死時，他們會擦亮我們的骸骨。

一九九四年十月

〔註：中國大陸，每天有一百五十名合法移民和數目不明的
非法移民進入香港。大牛是香港的五百元鈔票。許多非法
移民都當臨時工，有的則淪為罪犯。〕

Even in dwindling countryside
she'll be svelte in her green track suit
and her sports shoes will be costlier
than any trousseau for a village bride.

I'll stroll my city streets as sun begins to fade
I'll smoke long cigarettes between my teeth
and from a pure gold chain around my neck
will hang her heart of precious jade.

I'll master the use of portable phones
and I'll carry brown notes but no I/D.
Our kids will go to a school abroad,
but when we die, they'll polish our bones.

October 1994

[Note: 150 legal immigrants come into Hong Kong each day
from the P.R.C., as well as unknown numbers of illegal P.R.C.
immigrants. Brown bills in local currency are $500 H.K. Many
illegals are casual labourers and some are criminals.]

紫荊樹

香港之蘭樹
一行行佇立以待。
雨後的花
染白帶紅
閃亮如巧手精製玻璃。
樹上碩葉青翠——
然令人訝異：
竟有黃葉片片
在此暮春時分
垂首茫然

恰似盛暑未至
已待秋臨。

ORCHID TREES

The Hong Kong orchid trees
stand waiting in their rows.
Their flowers gleam after rain
as glass hand-blown
delicately tinted white and pink.
Their big leaves are green.
But something strange...
some curl yellow with fatigue
and hang there uncertain
in these last days of Spring

as if waiting for Fall
before Summer turns up her oven's heat.

顫楊

秋天，有一隻纖手，
伸出長長的手指，
在明淨的溪裡
淘著一片片的金子。
我在清涼的溪底仰望，
盈眸盡是水光和金光閃爍。

THE ASPEN

In Autumn a delicate hand
stretches out its long fingers,
washing piece upon piece of gold.
As I look up from the bottom of the cool, clear stream,
light of water and gold glitters and my eyes brim with light.

我怕霜降前就老去

怎麼我的心事如水，
未到白露就流入蒼茫？
蒼茫外有我久張的眼睛，
疲倦，惶惑，像兩口古井，
在蝙蝠崇人的翼下害怕天黑，
日落前在斷垣和白茅間
等一個遙遠的黎明。

隔著大河，南岸無聲向北；
北岸無聲等一葉小舟
載失散的族人歸來，
淚光中細辨久違的容貌；
等一道橋，即使簡陋，
接通令人傷心的天塹；
讓一個久被流放的孽子
風雨後趁月色趕路回家，
戰兢著，呀的一聲推門，
探首屋內，一聲長嘆後
透過淚光重認荒蕪的院落；
然後跪下，嘴唇哆嗦，
伸出震顫的雙手，在月光裡
閉目撫摩祖先的神位……

但面北，我怕霜降前就老去，
一尊石像那樣，立在山巔，
獨對天地的空闊和寂寞，
更怕冥冥越過千山的風雨
從遠處帶來暮色的淒絕。

一九七八年八月三十一日

106

I FEAR I MAY GROW OLD BEFORE FROST FALL

Why do my thoughts, like water,
before White Dew has ever come,
flow into the vast emptiness?
Beyond emptiness my long-awakened eyes,
weary, perplexed, like two ancient wells
beneath the evil wings of bats, fearful of nightfall,
in the hour before sunset,
amid broken walls and the lalang grass,
await a distant dawn.

Across the wide river, the southern bank looks north in silence.
In silence the northern bank awaits a small boat
bringing home the scattered clansmen,
scrutinizing through the sheen of tears faces long missed;
awaits a bridge, even if roughly built,
to span the heart-breaking divide,
so that after the storm the unworthy son, long exiled,
can hasten home by the light of the moon:
trembling, push open the creaking door,
gaze into the house and, with a long sigh,
try to know again through tears the ruined courtyard;
then, kneeling down, lips quivering,
stretch out his trembling hands, close his eyes,
and touch the shrine of his ancestors under the moon...

But gazing north, I fear I may grow old before Frost Fall,
standing atop the mountain like a stone figure,
alone with the vastness and solitude of heaven and earth,
fearful of the storms
that sweep darkly across immensities of mountains,
bringing with them from afar the bleak despair of dusk.

[Note: White Dew is the fifteenth solar term in the traditional
Chinese calendar, while Frost Fall is the eighteenth.]

藝術與眞理

我尋覓的藝術恰似石頭
經得起霜侵日曬
成形於往昔
開探於今日，宛如珍寶
閃耀著眞理的光輝
尖銳如彎彎利齒
深嵌於無語的顎骨中

ART AND TRUTH

I seek an art like stone,
enduring frost and sun,
formed by the past
yet new-mined like a gem
ablaze with truth
sharp as the curving tooth
stuck in a mute jawbone.

仙語

銀河風起，我就掛起輕帆，
訪你於下游。星槎漂過
魚紋般的細浪時，
我遙望兩岸紛紛下落的楓葉，
想起了采石磯和赤壁翫月的日子；
想起你如何離開曲江頭，
到終南山隱居，靜看梅林中的舞鶴。
滿天水色，星嶼散列如汀洲，
上面住著銀河的列仙。
過天津，繼續航向下游；
水迴竹林處，熟悉的笛聲傳來——
啊，我知道，你已擺好了棋盤。

到最後一子下完，
你我的肘邊，又不知
滅了多少星星，
亮了多少星星。

AN IMMORTAL SPEAKS

When the wind rises on the Silver River,
I'll hoist my light sails
and come downstream to visit you.
As my celestial boat drifts across scale-like ripples
I'll watch the maple leaves
fall on the distant shores
and remember the days when we laughed aloud
under the moon at the Gorgeous Rock and the Red Cliff.

I will remember how you left the Serpentine
for Zhongnan Mountain to live as a recluse
to watch the dancing cranes in the plum grove.
Amidst the light of the waters that wash the heavens,
starry islets spread like spits of land
on which immortals of the Silver River live.
Sailing past the Ford of Heaven,
I continue my voyage downstream.
Just as the water vanishes behind a bamboo grove,
I hear the familiar sound of a bamboo flute...
Ah, I know you have already set out the chessboard.

In the time it takes to reach our last move
how many more stars at our elbows
will have burnt themselves out,
how many more been lit?

風暴與鳥

颱風把滂沱大雨
摔過我們的山與洶湧的海
此時於此屋裡
我在燈暈下聆聽
悲喜相搏的樂聲

緩慢憂鬱的旋律
由奇異的欣悅取代
彷彿柴可夫斯基
以盈盈淚眼在微笑演奏。

我腦海裡的音樂屬於
一個活著的靈魂
及其所感所受。

我遭驅受摧
一如候鳥
失落在風暴滿佈的雲堆下。

一九九五年十月二日

112

STORM AND BIRD

Outside the typhoon shakes the sheeted rain
across the mountain and the crested sea
while in our room
I listen in the glow of lamps
to this music of two opposing moods

and the slow melancholy lilt
gives way to curious joy
as if with brimming eyes
Tchaikovsky smiled and played.

The music in my head
is of a living soul
and everything it feels.

I'm buffeted and driven
like some migrating bird
lost beneath the storm-filled clouds.

2 October 1995

光

我欣賞你將現未現時的神采：
來時從不張揚，更不必喧囂；
只是靜靜地溢出，自水平線下，
像紅瑪瑙融化，流過濕涼的藍水晶；
流入蘆葦叢裡，喚醒酣睡的漁人，
催他們鼓棹衝入東方的煙水。
我欣賞你在大地未醒時
踏著萬山的濕嶺赫然而來，
昧爽中奪目的金披肩
拂過還沒有天鵝蹤影的內陸湖，
拂過羊群還未出現的大草原，
在矢石升不到的高空
觸著雲雀無忌的胸膛。
我欣賞你夜靜時照白打穀場；
在深山照白澗水和石壁；
也欣賞你傲然在夜空獨行。
我欣賞你像美人的耳墜，
在天河兩岸丁丁東東地輕搖；
或像脫弦的利矢閃著青芒
霍霍霍射入宇宙的曠絕。
然而，我最欣賞的，
是你在黑夜的咆哮。
欣賞你狼嗥虎嘯時
屹然獨立在黑夜的中央，
安慰所有驚惶的瞳孔。

114

LIGHT

I hail the latent aura of your coming.
When you arrive, you do not exult,
never create a din,
but silent, well above the horizon,
like red agate melting, you stream
over cool blue crystal,
flooding into thickets of reeds, waking the fishermen,
urging them to row into the misty waters of the east.
I hail you when in full majesty
you stride across crowds of dewy mountains before earth wakes.
In dawn's dimness, your golden cape
trails over hidden lakes that have never seen swan,
above vast prairies, where flocks will come to graze,
touches the fearless chest of the skylark
at heights slings and bows cannot reach.
I hail you when you shine white
upon threshing floors in night's silence;
white on brooks and on cliffs deep in the mountains,
when, alone and proud, you traverse the night sky.
I hail you when you sparkle on the banks of the River of Heaven,
twinkling like the ear-rings of a beautiful woman,
or flashing green like an arrow loosed from the bow,
shoot to the farthest wilderness of the universe.
Yet above all I hail
your roaring in the night,
standing alone, unshaken in the very heart of darkness,
amidst howling wolves and ravening tigers,
comforting every fearful eye.

長夜漫漫，當堅固的堡壘
在黑暗中妥協、投降，
稜稜的輪廓溶入暗影；
當幽靈和鬼魅四出祟人，
日間的英雄像海邊的野草，
潮漲時紛紛俯伏隱身；
當灰衣客身子一晃，
紛紛投入了夜色，無蹤無影；
天地間剩下你，立場最分明；
天地間，唯有你，熊熊在長嘯，
因為，天地間，只有你
才是真正的勇士。

一九八二年六月八日

In long-drawn-out nights, when the strongest defence yields,
surrenders in the dark,
its sharp features melting into shadow,
when spectres and ghouls go haunting,
when daylight's heroes like weeds on the beach
lie prostrate and huddle when tides rise,
when grey-clad hordes
flash by and hurl themselves into the night,
leaving no trace,
you alone remain, between heaven and earth,
staunchly there, for all to see.
Yes, between heaven and earth, you are the only hero,
ablaze and roaring in your flames.

8 June 1982

颼過中國的暴風雨

在千百萬騎自行車的群眾
和邊界楞楞的群山之上，
電光舔著黑穹。

一次，又一次，龍舌
以火焰的白字
拂擦著黑夜之書。

一九九二年一月

STORM ACROSS CHINA

above the cycling millions
and the stark hills of the frontier
lightning licks a black sky

again and yet again a dragon's tongue
brushes the book of night
with white characters of fire

January 1992

姜安道作品

POEMS BY ANDREW PARKIN

姜安道作品（鳴謝）：

英文原作：中大校刊（一九九一年夏）：《在中文大學》；
香港電台第三台廣播（一九九三年三月）：《在啓德國際機
場降落》；香港筆會刊物（一九九三年一月）：《四寶》；
《人文學刊》第三期（一九九四年六月）：《香港短歌》；
《吐露燈：一九九三》（香港：香港中文大學逸夫書院，一
九九四年）：《愛在薄暮》；《翻譯季刊》第二期（一九九
五年八月）：《山巒和海港》（一、二）。

中譯：《香港文學》月刊第七十九期（一九九一年七月）：
《在中文大學》；《翻譯季刊》第二期（一九九五年八
月）：《在啓德國際機場降落》、《四寶》、《香港短
歌》、《山巒和海港》（一、二）；《香港文學》月刊第一
四三期（一九九六年十一月）：《另一伊甸》、《藝術與眞
理》、《晨光熹微時》、《拼圖》、《給一名巴黎女子的情
書》、《紫荊樹》。

ACKNOWLEDGEMENTS:
Andrew Parkin

The English originals: "At Chinese University" appeared in *The Chinese University Newsletter* (Summer, 1991); "Descent to Kai Tak International Airport" was broadcast on RTHK Radio 3, March, 1993; "Four Treasures" appeared in *PEN* (*Hong Kong*) *Broadsheet* (January, 1993); "Hong Kong Tanka" appeared in *The Humanities Bulletin* No. 3 (June, 1994); "Love at Dusk" appeared in *Tolo Lights 1993* (Hong Kong: Shaw College, CUHK, 1994), "Mountain and Harbour" (I, II) appeared in *Translation Quarterly*, No. 2 (August, 1995).

The Chinese translations: "Descent to Kai Tak International Airport", "Four Treasures", "Hong Kong Tanka", "Mountain and Harbour" (I, II) appeared in *Translation Quarterly*, No. 2 (August, 1995); "Another Eden", "Art and Truth", "In the Lesser Dark", "Jigsaw", "Storm and Bird", "Love Letter to a Woman in Paris", "Orchid Trees", and "Typhoon" appeared in *Hong Kong Literature Monthly*, No. 143 (November, 1996).

黃國彬作品

POEMS BY LAURENCE WONG

黃國彬作品（鳴謝）：

中文原作：《息壤歌》（香港：學津書店，一九八零年）：《小夜曲的聯想》（一、二)）、《我的詩》、《拉二胡》；《翡冷翠的多天》（香港：山邊社，一九八三年）：《雨夜狂想》；《吐露港日月》（香港：學津書店，一九八三年）：《光》、《永樂大鐘》、《熱帶魚》、《當我的夢如無際的疆土展開》；《微茫秒忽》（香港：天琴出版社，一九九三年）：《仙語》、《秋懷》、《只要你站得久》、《春》；《地劫》（香港：詩風出版社，一九七七年）：《狂吟》、《拍照》；《臨江仙》（香港：天琴出版社，一九九三年）：《望江南》、《大寒》。

英譯：《譯叢》第十九、二十期（一九八三年春季、秋季合刊）：《我的詩》、《拉二胡》、《狂吟》、《拍照》、《翠鳥》；《譯叢》第二十九、三十期（一九八八年春季、秋季合刊）：《小夜曲的聯想》（一、二）、《我怕霜降前就老去》、《光》、《雨夜狂想》、《永樂大鐘》、《熱帶魚》；《在海港最藍處》，姜安道編（香港：牛津大學出版社，一九九五年）：《只要你站得久》、《望江南》、《秋懷》、《春》、《大寒》。

126

ACKNOWLEDGEMENTS:
Laurence Wong

The Chinese originals: "Free Associations on a Serenade" (I, II), "My Poem", "Playing the Erhu" are from *Song of the Flood-Taming Loam* (Hong Kong: Learner's Bookstore, 1980); "Rhapsody on a Rainy Night" is from *Winter in Florence* (Hong Kong: Sunbeam Press, 1983); "Light", "The Great Bell of Yongle", "Tropical Fish", "When My Dream Spreads Like Some Boundless Land" are from *Days and Months at Tolo Harbour* (Hong Kong: Learner's Bookstore, 1983); "An Immortal Speaks", "Autumn Thoughts", "Just Stand There Long Enough", "Spring" are from *The Dim Crepuscular Gleam* (Hong Kong: Lyra Press, 1993); "Raving Song", "Taking a Picture" are from *Plague of the Earth* (Hong Kong: Shih Feng Press, 1977); "Gazing South", "Great Cold" are from *The Immortal by the River* (Hong Kong: Lyra Press, 1993).

The English translations: "My Poem", "Playing the Erhu", "Raving Song", "Taking a Picture", "The Kingfisher" appeared in *Renditions* Nos. 19, 20 (Spring and Autumn, 1983); "Free Associations on a Serenade "(I, II)", "I Fear I May Grow Old Before Frost Fall", "Light", "Rhapsody on a Rainy Night", "The Great Bell of Yongle", "Tropical Fish" appeared in *Renditions* Nos. 29, 30 (Spring and Autumn, 1988); "Just Stand There Long Enough", "Gazing South", "Autumn Thoughts", "Spring", "Great Cold" appeared in *From the Bluest Part of the Harbour* (Hong Kong: Oxford University Press, 1995).

譯者與所譯作品一覽表

吳兆朋

中譯：《在啓德國際機場降落》；《四寶》；港畔（一、二）；《香港短歌》；《山巒和海港》（一、二）。

英譯：《秋懷》；《望江南》；《大寒》；《只要你站得久》；《春》。

金聖華

中譯：《另一伊甸》；《藝術與眞理》；《晨光熹微時》；《拼圖》；《給一名巴黎女子的情書》；《紫荊樹》；《風暴與鳥》；《颶風》。

莫詠賢

英譯：《我的詩》；《拉二胡》；《拍照》；《狂吟》。

黃國彬

中譯：《太空人》；《在中文大學》；《閃電拆開黑穹的針腳》；《愛在薄暮》；《在下臨吐露港的山上》；《寄跑馬地的明信片》；《睡海》；《非法移民之歌》；《颶過中國的暴風雨》；《四季卷軸——致劉國松》。

英譯：《仙語》；《小夜曲的聯想》（一、二）；《我怕霜降前就老去》；《光》；《雨夜狂想》；《永樂大鐘》；《翠鳥》；《熱帶魚》；《寂寞》；《當我的夢如無際的疆土展開》。

TRANSLATORS AND TRANSLATIONS

EVANGELINE ALMBERG translated into Chinese:

Descent to Kai Tak; Four Treasures; Harbourside (I, II); Hong Kong Tanka; Mountain and Harbour (I, II).

into English:

Autumn Thoughts; Gazing South; Great Cold; Just Stand There Long Enough; Spring.

SERENA JIN translated into Chinese:

Another Eden; Art and Truth; In the Lesser Dark; Jigsaw; Love Letter to a Woman in Paris; Orchid Trees; Storm and Bird; Typhoon.

MOK WING-YIN translated into English:

My Poem; Playing the Erhu; Taking a Picture; Raving Song.

LAURENCE WONG translated into Chinese:

Astronaut; At Chinese University; Lightning Unstitches the Dark Sky; Love at Dusk; On a Mountain above Tolo Harbour; Postcard to Happy Valley; Sleeping Sea; Song of an Illegal Immigrant; Storm Across China; The Four Seasons Handscroll.

into English:

An Immortal Speaks; Free Associations on a Serenade (I, II); I Fear I May Grow Old Before Frost Fall; Light; Rhapsody on a Rainy Night; The Great Bell of Yongle; The Kingfisher; Tropical Fish; When My Dream Spreads Like Some Boundless Land.

作者簡介

姜安道，加拿大籍，一九三七年在英國出生；劍橋大學文學士、文學碩士；布里斯托爾大學戲劇科哲學博士。六十年代中期在香港一所中學任教。一九七零年移居加拿大，在不列顛哥倫比亞大學教英語。當時所寫的詩，大都在加拿大發表。姜安道是加拿大作家協會、加拿大筆會、香港筆會會員，也是加拿大愛爾蘭研究學會永遠名譽會員。已出版多本學術著作、兩本詩集（《蛛網中的舞者》、《橫濱日、京都夜》），並發表多篇論文。所編的香港中詩英譯《在海港最藍處》，最近由牛津大學出版社出版。姜安道於一九九一年返港，任香港中文大學英文系講座教授。此外，他也是中文大學逸夫書院院務委員會委員、中文大學讚詞撰寫及宣讀人、香港加拿大研究學會創辦人兼主席。

黃國彬，一九四六年在香港出生；香港大學英文與翻譯科文學士、英文科碩士、多倫多大學哲學博士。過去二十年先後在香港中文大學英文系、香港大學英文與比較文學系、加拿大約克大學語言、文學及語言學系任教；目前為香港嶺南學院翻譯系教授兼主任。已出版十一本詩集、五本散文集、六本評論集、一本譯論，並發表多篇中文、英文、法文、意大利文、德文、西班牙文詩歌的翻譯。

ABOUT THE POETS

ANDREW PARKIN, born in 1937 in England, received his B.A. and M.A. in English from the University of Cambridge. His Ph.D. in Drama is from Bristol University. He taught in a school in Hong Kong in the mid-sixties and then emigrated to Canada in 1970, teaching English at the University of British Columbia, as well as writing and publishing his poetry, mainly in Canada. He is a Canadian citizen and a member of the Canadian Writers' Union and P.E.N. Canada as well as the Hong Kong chapter of P.E.N. An honorary life member of the Canadian Association for Irish Studies, he has published several academic books, numerous essays, and two books of poetry, *Dancers in a Web* and *Yokohama Days, Kyoto Nights*. His most recent book is an anthology of Hong Kong Chinese poetry in English, *From the Bluest Part of the Harbour* (O.U.P.). He returned to Hong Kong in 1991 to take up the Chair of English at the Chinese University, where he is a Fellow of Shaw College and University Orator. He is founder president of the Association for Canadian Studies in Hong Kong.

LAURENCE WONG was born in 1946 in Hong Kong and received his B.A. in English and Translation as well as his M. Phil. in English from the University of Hong Kong. His Ph.D. is from the University of Toronto. Over the last twenty years he has taught in the English Department at the Chinese University of Hong Kong, the Department of English Studies and Comparative Literature at the University of Hong Kong, the Department of Languages, Literatures, and Linguistics at York University, Ontario, and most recently as University Reader and Head of the Department of Translation at Lingnan College in Hong Kong. His publications include eleven books of poetry, five collections of "lyrical essays", six collections of critical essays, one collection of essays on translation, and translations of Chinese, English, French, Italian, German, and Spanish poetry.

譯者簡介

吳兆朋，香港大學英文系學士。斯德哥爾摩大學漢學博士。現任香港中文大學翻譯系副教授。著作包括中英文詩歌的英中翻譯；目前的研究範圍包括斯堪的納維亞文學中譯。

金聖華，香港中文大學翻譯系教授兼主任；一九九零至一九九二年任香港翻譯學會主席。已出版多本創作和有關翻譯的論著（如《英譯中：英漢翻譯概論》、《英語新辭辭彙》）、多本文學作品的翻譯（如麥克勒絲的《小酒館的悲歌》、康拉德的《海隅逐客》、厄戴克的《約翰·厄戴克小說選集》、布邁恪的《石與影》和《黑娃的故事》）。多年來，金聖華一直致力於提高翻譯在香港和大陸的地位，並以中文譯介英國、加拿大、美國、法國的重要文學作品。

莫詠賢，香港大學文學士、文學碩士、哲學博士；專門研究中國古典詩歌和中國古典詩歌的翻譯；目前在香港中文大學翻譯系任教。

ABOUT THE TRANSLATORS

EVANGELINE S.P. ALMBERG read English at the University of Hong Kong and received her Ph.D. in Sinology from the University of Stockholm. Her publications include translations of Chinese poetry into English and vice versa. She is presently an Associate Professor in the Department of Translation of the Chinese University of Hong Kong. Her current research interests include studies in Chinese translations of Scandinavian literature.

SERENA JIN is Professor and Chairman of the Department of Translation at the Chinese University of Hong Kong. She was President of the Hong Kong Translation Society (1990-92). Her publications include creative writing, books on translation, such as *Principles of Translation* and *A Glossary of New English,* and translations of literary texts, such as Carson McCullers' *The Ballad of the Sad Café,* Joseph Conrad's *An Outcast of the Islands,* John Updike's *Short Stories of John Updike,* and Michael Bullock's *Stone and Shadow* and *The Story of Noire.* Her main areas of interest are the promotion of translation in Hong Kong and China and the translation of significant English, Canadian, American, and French literary works into Chinese.

MOK WING-YIN received her B.A., M. Phil. and Ph.D. from the University of Hong Kong, specializing in the study and translation of Chinese classical poetry. She now teaches in the Department of Translation at the Chinese University of Hong Kong.

後記

在舉世放眼全球、大量移民在洲與洲之間遷徙的年代，我們當中有許多人，常會發覺自己生活在國家與國家、語言與語言、文化與文化之間。我們所處的狀態，可能就是香港評論家艾克巴・阿巴斯所謂的「後文化」狀態。二十年來，香港的歷史一直處於關鍵時刻，一直叫人驚異不置。姜安道和黃國彬的《香港詩歌》，就表現了這段歷史所引發的許多感覺和稍縱即逝的意念、心境、冥思。兩位詩人都是加拿大籍，目前居於香港，卻屬於不同的族裔。本書把他們的作品結為一集，以中英對照形式出版，是一項獨特的創舉。今年是香港主權回歸中國、香港人組成香港特別行政區政府的一年。就在這樣的一年，本書向讀者展示了香港在詩人感覺中的過去和此地此時，展示了地方、城市、國家的生動美感；讓他們知道，這個「海膽城市」有什麼樣的魅力，可以叫遊客從亞洲其他地區——甚至亞洲以外的世界——一再舊地重遊。

由於作品的特別編排，兩位詩人可以互相對話，詩作與詩作、中文與英文、譯者與詩人、詩人與譯者也可以彼此交談。這種對話，是詩的想像與兩種文化的對話。兩種文化，又由第三種文化，即加拿大文化——全球後文化的一部分——聯繫在一起。

香港是個重要城市，叫人踔厲昂揚。其所以如此，不完全因為它是活力、財富以及各種時尚的發電機，也不僅因為它處於歷史時刻，而因為它是現在和將來交會、殖民（甚至後殖民）色彩為亞洲現代特色急劇取代之地，此刻正蓄勢待發，要一飛沖天，飛入二十一世紀。每天消逝的事物，會無可避免地引起懷舊之情；生活在中國的邊緣，會無可避免地感到不安。這本詩集，多少向讀者表現了這兩種感受。不過，置身於此時此地，本身就是一種刺激。這本詩集，也多少給讀者傳達了這樣的經驗。

134

AFTERWORD

In the age of globalism and mass migrations from one continent to another, many of us find ourselves living in between countries, in between languages, in between cultures. We may be in a state called "postculture" by Hong Kong critic Ackbar Abbas. These Hong Kong Poems by Andrew Parkin and Laurence Wong express many of the sensations, fleeting ideas, moods, and meditations that come from the astonishing and crucial history of Hong Kong over the last twenty years. By putting together two Canadian poets, both residents of Hong Kong but of different ethnic origins, and offering their poems in both English and Chinese, this book does something unique. In the year when Hong Kong returns to Chinese sovereignty and the government of the Special Administrative Region will be made up of Hong Kong people, the book offers poets' perceptions of what Hong Kong was and is right now. It gives a vivid sense of the beauty of place, city and country, and the fascination of the "sea urchin city" that keeps tourists from the rest of Asia and the rest of the world coming back.

The arrangement of the poems creates a dialogue between the two poets, with poem speaking to poem, Chinese language speaking to English language, translators speaking to poets and poets to translators. This is the poetic imagination in dialogue with two cultures, united in a third, Canada, which is part of a global postculture.

Hong Kong is a significant and exciting place, not merely because it's a dynamo of energy, wealth, and fashion, not just because of its historical moment, but because it's a place where the present meets the future, where the colonial and even the post-colonial is being rapidly replaced by Asian modernity, poised to soar into the twenty-first century. This book offers some of the inevitable nostalgia for that which disappears each day, some of the inevitable apprehension attached to living on the edge of China, but also some of the sheer excitement of being there, now!